THE HISTORY OF THE CALENDAR

BY BARBARA A. SOMERVILL

▲ 4236 B.C.
Egyptians record their
first calendar year.

▼ 45 B.C.
Julius Caesar orders that
the new Julian calendar
be used as a standard for
tracking time.

C. JULIUS CÆSAR.

▲ A.D. 1582
The Gregorian calendar
becomes the standard for
tracking time.

5000 B.C.	4000	3000	2000	1000	A.D. 0	1000	2000

Content Adviser: Gary M. Feinma[n] . . . [Anthropo]logy, The Field Museum, Chicago, Illinois

THE CHILD'S WORLD® • CHANHASSEN, MINNESOTA

The Child's World®

Published in the United States of America by The Child's World®
PO Box 326 • Chanhassen, MN 55317-0326 • 800-599-READ • www.childsworld.com

ACKNOWLEDGMENTS
The Child's World®: Mary Berendes, Publishing Director

Editorial Directions, Inc.: E. Russell Primm, Editorial Director; Katie Marsico, Managing Editor and Line Editor; Judith Shiffer, Assistant Editor; Rory Mabin and Caroline Wood, Editorial Assistants; Susan Hindman, Copy Editor; Jennifer Martin, Proofreader; Judith Frisbee, Peter Garnham, Olivia Nellums, Chris Simms, and Stephen Carl Wender, Fact Checkers; Tim Griffin/IndexServ, Indexer; Cian Loughlin O'Day, Photo Researcher; Linda S. Koutris, Photo Selector

The Design Lab: Kathleen Petelinsek, Design and Art Production; Julia Goozen, Art Production Assistant

PHOTOS
Cover/frontispiece: left, center, right—Bettmann/Corbis.

Interior: 5—Jim Cummins/Corbis; 7, 26—Bettmann/Corbis; 9—Werner Forman/Art Resource, NY; 10—Burke/Triolo Productions/Brand X Pictures/Getty Images; 11—Giraudon/Art Resource, NY; 12—Gianni Dagli Orti/Corbis; 15—Erich Lessing/Art Resource, NY; 17—George H. H. Huey/Corbis; 18—Egyptian Museum, Cairo; 20, 24—Library of Congress; 21, 22—The Granger Collection; 25—Snark/Art Resource, NY; 28—Reuters/Corbis; 29—Warner Bros./Getty Images.

LIBRARY OF CONGRESS CATALOGING-IN-PUBLICATION DATA
Somervill, Barbara A.
  The history of the calendar / by Barbara Somervill.
    p. cm. — (Our changing world—the timeline library)
  Includes index.
  ISBN 1-59296-436-2 (library bound : alk. paper)
  1. Calendar—History—Juvenile literature. I. Title. II. Series.
  CE6.S66 2006
  529'.3—dc22   2005024783

TABLE OF CONTENTS

WHAT YEAR IS IT?

Mr. Hoffman smiled at the class. "What year were you born?" he asked. Every hand in the class shot up. Mr. Hoffman called on Chen Qi.

"I was born in the year of the boar, 4693," Chen Qi said. Everyone in the class laughed. The year 4693! Chen Qi didn't know what he was talking about.

Mr. Hoffman nodded. "Chen Qi is correct. Now, Rachel, tell us what year you were born."

Rachel answered, "I was born in 5755."

Before the class could react, Mr. Hoffman raised his hand. "Chen Qi told us the year of his birth according to the Chinese calendar. Rachel's birth year is based on the Jewish calendar. Did you know that different cultures follow different calendars? There are forty different types of calendars being used today. Different calendars start their years at different times, have different names for months and days, and even contain different numbers of days in a year."

He concluded, "For homework this week, I want you to become calendar detectives. Find a calendar from a different culture. Write a story based on something connected to that calendar. You can use any calendar except the one we normally use . . . the Gregorian calendar."

"Gregorian calendar?" muttered Brittany. "We use the calendar from Frankie's Garage."

Are you the same age as everyone in your class? Depending on which calendar system you use, different people in your class could each say they were born in a different year!

CHAPTER ONE

A DAY, A MONTH, A YEAR

Thousands of years ago, people paid attention to the sun's rising and setting. They noticed the moon as it rose in the darkness—full, round, and glowing. After a few sunrises (later called days), the moon's size would decrease until it completely disappeared. Then the moon would reappear in the sky, a sliver of light against the blackness. It would grow full and round again as more sunrises passed.

Early people marked the sunrises by carving notches, or V-shaped cuts, on a bone. When the moon shone round in the sky once again, that event was marked with a larger, deeper notch. This carved bone may have been the first calendar. Sunrises marked the days. The full moon marked the months. The days and months probably had no names at that point.

Humans keep track of days and months by making notches on a bone.

ca. 10,000 B.C.

The ancient city of Jericho is built.

4236 B.C.: THE FIRST TRUE CALENDAR

The first true calendar was probably developed in Egypt. Someone noticed that Sirius, the Dog Star, rose next to the sun every 365 days. Sirius appeared in the **constellation** Canis Major. The star's appearance in that spot matched the most important event in the Egyptian year—the flooding of the Nile River.

Egypt's Nile River provided water, fish, and a transportation route. Each year, the Nile flooded at about the same time—July 1 on

Egyptians use a calendar (right) to record the passing of a year.

4236 B.C.

Mesopotamians develop the wheel.

modern-day calendars. The flood poured life-giving water, enriched soil, and nutrients across the dry Egyptian land. Because everyone depended on this flood, it was considered an important date and marked the beginning of the Egyptian year.

The Jewish, or Hebrew, calendar dates back nearly as far as the Egyptian calendar—to 3760 B.C. The Jewish calendar is still in use. The date listed as 1 A.M. (*Anno Mundi,* or "Year of the World") marks the beginning of the Jewish faith. The Jewish calendar has two types of years: ordinary years and leap years. Ordinary years have 12 months and 353 to 355 days. Leap years have 13 months and 383 to 385 days. The Jewish year begins with

3760 B.C.

The Jewish calendar is created, marking the start of Judaism.

Copper tools are used in present-day Iran.

the religious holiday Rosh Hashanah, which usually occurs in mid-September. Jewish days begin at sunset.

3114 B.C.: THE WORLD BEGINS . . . ACCORDING TO THE EARLY MIDDLE AMERICANS

Mexico, Guatemala, Belize, and parts of Honduras and El Salvador all make up what is called Middle America. Thousands of miles from Egypt, the peoples of Middle America created their own calendar. Their calendar

The world is created, according to Middle American calendars (right).

3114 B.C.

The Early Dynasty Period begins in Egypt.

dated from when they believed the world began. That happened in 3114 B.C., according to our modern calendar. By the last centuries B.C.E., these Middle Americans, including the Maya, used three calendars—the Long Count, the *tzolkin*, and the *haab*.

The Maya Long Count started with the first day of creation and counted upward. This calendar system was divided into units that stood for various numbers of days. But the Long Count often proved too difficult for everyday use.

The Maya also had two other calendars. The tzolkin religious calendar covered 260 days. It consisted of a blend of numbers from one through thirteen and

ca. 3000 B.C.

The abacus (left) is first
seen in southwest Asia.

contained twenty names for various weeks. A week would be written "eight *chiccan*" or "six *lamat*."

The civil (daily) calendar, called haab, included 365 days. The haab and the tzolkin came together every fifty-two years, when the cycle began again.

CA. 3000 B.C.: THE SUMERIAN CALENDAR

In about 3000 B.C., the Sumerians of the Tigris-Euphrates valley (present-day Iraq) created a twelve-month calendar. Each month had thirty days, and each day had twelve units that were roughly equal to two of our hours. The

Sumerians develop a calendar (right) containing thirty-day months.

ca. 3000 B.C.

People in the Middle East begin using bronze tools.

11

twelve units were further divided into thirty smaller periods that covered about four minutes each.

But the Sumerian calendar had some built-in problems. Their year only had 360 days. Today, scientists know that the **tropical year,** the year on which our calendar is based, has 365 days. The Sumerian calendar was five days short. After six years, the calendar would be a month off. After thirty-six years, the "harvest month" would come half a year earlier than it was supposed to—at planting time. These problems made the Sumerian calendar confusing.

ca. 3760 B.C.

The first schools are established in Mesopotamia, and students use cuneiform (right) as their writing system.

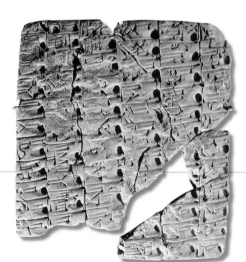

CHAPTER TWO

FROM THE YEAR OF THE MONKEY TO THE MEDICINE WHEEL

O ther cultures developed calendars as well. The Chinese calendar uses animal names for each year—boar, rat, ox, tiger, hare, dragon, snake, horse, ram, monkey, rooster, and dog. The Chinese believe that a person's personality is determined by the year of birth. For example, a child born in the year of the dragon might become a powerful leader who is fierce, determined, and strong. The animals that make up the calendar are also part of the Chinese **zodiac.** Like the Jewish calendar, the Chinese calendar is still used.

According to Chinese legends, Emperor Huangdi established an early calendar in 2637 B.C. During the rule of Emperor Huangdi, Chinese calendars began following a sixty-year cycle. Each of the sixty years was named, just as

The Chinese begin using a sixty-year calendar cycle.

2637 B.C.

The Step Pyramid is built in Egypt.

> "EVEN THE EMPEROR HIMSELF
> CANNOT BUY ANOTHER DAY."
> —CHINESE PROVERB

each was tied to one of the twelve zodiac signs. About 300 years later, Emperor Yao adjusted the Chinese calendar.

A new Chinese calendar cycle began in February 1984. The first cycle year is called *bing yin,* and the first month is *gui chou.* But the Chinese did not count their calendar years continuously. They skipped a few—and now the calendar is sixty years off!

Chinese years have traditionally been divided into twenty-four periods, which are all connected to the seasons. Spring periods include Rain Water, Excited Insects, and Heavy Rains. Summer features Great Heat and Grain in Ear. Fall has White Dew and Falling Frost, while winter includes Heavy Snow and Severe Cold.

2357 B.C.

Emperor Yao adjusts the
Chinese calendar.

Tangun founds the first
Korean kingdom.

CA. 1750 B.C.: WEEKS, HOURS, MINUTES, SECONDS

The Babylonians lived near the Sumerians. They were a more recent culture and developed a more accurate calendar. The Babylonian calendar included twelve months based on a **lunar** cycle. Babylonian months alternated between twenty-nine and thirty days. This system resulted in a year with only 354 days. To even out their year, the Babylonians inserted a "leap month," called *iti dirig*. This leap month guaranteed that the "harvest month" actually occurred at harvest time.

Babylonians switch to a calendar (right) that includes seven-day weeks, twenty-four-hour days, sixty-minute hours, and sixty-second minutes.

ca. 1750 B.C.

Babylonian king and lawmaker Hammurabi dies.

In about 1750 B.C., the Babylonians made some major changes in their timekeeping practices. They set up a seven-day week and named the days after the sun, the moon, and the five brightest stars in the sky. They divided days into twenty-four hours. Each hour lasted sixty minutes, and each minute contained sixty seconds. This means that the time segments we use today were created more than 3,750 years ago!

CA. A.D. 100: MEDICINE WHEELS ON THE GREAT PLAINS

More than two thousand years ago on the Great Plains of North America, the Plains Indians created a simple, nature-related method of tracking time. Their months

260 B.C.

Arabic numerals are first seen in India.

marked the changing shape of the moon. Each new moon was connected to some aspect of daily life such as hunting, planting, growing, and harvesting.

The Plains Indians also honored the sun and its importance in their lives. They built medicine wheels to measure the sun's position. The wheels were large circles of stones. Each wheel had stone spokes, which led to a large stone pile in the center. The wheel's outer rim contained stone piles in carefully chosen locations. When **vectors** were drawn from one pile to another, the lines pointed to major stars in the summer sky—Aldebaran, Sirius, and Rigel.

ca. A.D. 100

Plains tribes begin building medicine wheels (right).

Shadow puppets are created in China.

CHAPTER THREE

JULIUS CAESAR AND POPE GREGORY

The Roman Empire expanded to rule the world—at least most of Europe and North Africa. All roads led to Rome. All Romans used the same coins, paid the same taxes, and followed the same calendar.

But by the time of Julius Caesar, the Roman calendar was a mess. Roman senators played political games with the calendar. They added months so they could put off holding elections.

In 46 B.C., Caesar hired an **astronomer** named Sosigenes to develop a better calendar. The new calendar was based on the **solar** year. The new year began January 1 and included twelve months of regular, fixed lengths. Every four years, a leap day would follow the last day of February.

Julius Caesar orders that the new Julian calendar be used as a standard for tracking time.

45 B.C.

Ptolemy XV (right) is pharaoh of Egypt.

In 45 B.C., Caesar ordered that this new calendar be used as the standard for tracking time. The new Julian calendar added 80 days to that year, making it 445 days long. The year 45 B.C. was therefore known as the Year of Confusion.

A.D. 1347: BLACK DEATH STRIKES

In A.D. 1347, Pope Clement VI busily planned a new, improved calendar. He intended to replace the old system by 1349. Unfortunately for Clement, a ship landed in Messina, Sicily, carrying much more than silks and spices. The ship carried the bubonic plague—a deadly illness that came to be known as the Black Death.

During the next few years, 30 million Europeans

MONTH NAMES
BEFORE 700 B.C., THE ROMAN CALENDAR FEATURED TEN MONTHS. THE LAST FOUR MONTHS HAD NAMES RELATED TO NUMBERS. IN 700 B.C., TWO NEW MONTHS WERE ADDED TO THE CALENDAR, MOVING THE LAST FOUR MONTHS TO POSITIONS NINE THROUGH TWELVE. SUDDENLY, SEPTEMBER—WHICH MEANT "SEVENTH MONTH"—WAS THE NINTH MONTH! CAN YOU GUESS THE REAL MEANING OF OCTOBER, NOVEMBER, AND DECEMBER?

Pope Clement VI unsuccessfully attempts calendar reform.

A.D. 1347

The Black Death sweeps through Europe.

died a miserable, painful death. That equaled about one-third of Europe's total population. Priests and peasants, scholars and traders, children and grandfathers—no one was spared. When the Black Death finally came to an end, survivors had no interest in the calendar. Pope Clement's new system of tracking time became another victim of the Black Death.

1582: GREGORY'S CALENDAR

In 1512, Pope Julius II decided to fix the Julian calendar. Ever since people had started using the Julian calendar, each year had lost a few minutes. After more than 1,500 years, the Julian calendar was about 10 days off. Pope Julius called a meeting of astronomers, scientists, and mathemati-

1512

Christopher Columbus (left) travels to the New World.

cians. Before the council made any decisions, however, Pope Julius II died.

Pope Leo X took his place. He also wanted to repair the Julian calendar. He asked the kings and princes of Europe to send their smartest men to Rome to help. Astronomer Nicolaus Copernicus was asked for his help. Copernicus refused because he said that the exact length of the tropical year was not known. Until that fact was determined, he believed there was no point in trying to fix the calendar.

In the early 1570s, Pope Gregory XIII set up a committee to fix the calendar.

Pope Julius II attempts to fix the Julian calendar (right).

Michelangelo completes the ceiling of the Sistine Chapel.

Several years later, mathematician Christopher Clavius was asked to lead the group. Clavius was a Jesuit priest from Bavaria, Germany. Oddly, Clavius developed an accurate calendar, despite his belief that the Earth was the center of the universe.

In 1582, the Gregorian calendar went into action. To correct the problems with the Julian calendar, this new system skipped ten days. October 15 immediately followed October 4. The change was readily accepted in most Catholic countries such as Italy, Poland, Portugal, and Spain.

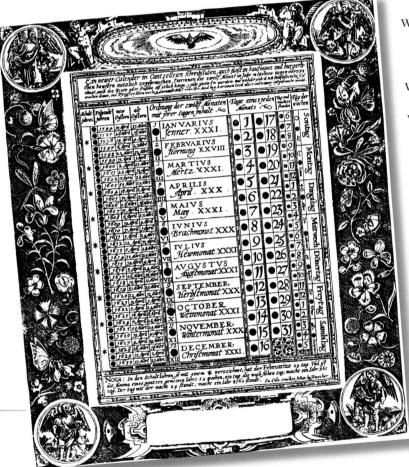

The Gregorian calendar (left) becomes the standard for tracking time.

1582

William Shakespeare marries Anne Hathaway in Stratford-upon-Avon.

CHAPTER FOUR

OUR MODERN CALENDAR

Although the Gregorian calendar was popular in Roman Catholic countries, not everyone adopted Pope Gregory's solution. Many Protestants refused to follow the new calendar. This meant that several European countries used a different calendar. A person traveled through time just by stepping over the border from Denmark to Germany!

Some countries struggled to correct these differences. For example, Sweden decided to drop one day every leap year, beginning in 1700 and lasting until 1740. This was not a success. Somehow, the Swedes forgot to skip the 1704 and 1708 leap days. Then they decided to return to the Julian calendar. To do this, they added an extra day to 1712 to get back the one they skipped in 1700. As a result, February 1712 ended up having thirty days! Such confusion!

Sweden tries to adapt to the Gregorian calendar by skipping leap days every four years.

1700

The clarinet is invented.

The Swedes managed to switch to the Gregorian calendar forty years later.

Great Britain and its colonies did not adopt the new calendar until 1752. To make the switch, all British colonies—including the future United States—jumped from September 2, 1752, to September 14, 1752.

1792: THE FRENCH REVOLUTIONARY CALENDAR

The Gregorian calendar would eventually become accepted throughout most of the world. For a while, however, other cultures continued developing different calendars.

In North America, Plains tribes kept calendar histories called winter counts. Every year, a **pictograph** of a

Great Britain and its colonies adopt a calendar system that skips from September 2 to September 14 during the first year it is used.

1752

Benjamin Franklin (left) invents the lightning rod.

special event would be added to a large animal skin covered with similar pictures. Each picture recalled a year in the tribe's history.

The French Revolution (1789–1799) affected the calendar used in France. The Revolutionary calendar began on September 22, 1792, which was 1 Vendemiaire, Year I. The new calendar had twelve months that each contained thirty days. Weeks lasted ten days. The months were named for sea-

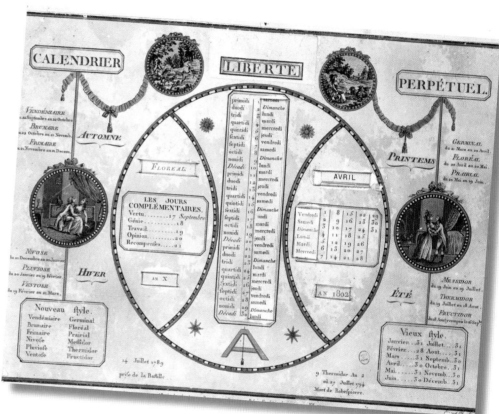

The French begin using the Revolutionary calendar (right).

1792

The first U.S. Mint opens and produces coins in Philadelphia.

sonal changes, such as *Florial* (blossoms) and *Messidor* (harvest).

By the 1900s, nearly all countries accepted the Gregorian system as the standard world calendar. In 1940, the Soviet Union became one of the last countries to adopt the Gregorian calendar. The Eastern Orthodox Church continues to use the Julian calendar. Although the church has voted on the issue several times, members still reject the Gregorian calendar.

1940

The Soviet Union finally accepts the Gregorian calendar.

The color television is first introduced (right).

CHAPTER FIVE

BETTER WAYS OF KEEPING TIME

There are many types of calendars and several different ways of tracking time's passage. Over milennia—periods of one thousand years—people have found more exact ways to measure time. But our calendar continues to need adjustment.

Three interesting time measurement systems include Julian time, sidereal time, and International Atomic Time. Julian dates resemble the Maya Long Count. The Julian count began on January 1, 4713 B.C. This system helps astronomers figure the number of days between two major **celestial** events, such as **eclipses** or passing comets.

International Atomic Time is kept at a number of atomic clock facilities. In 1972, timekeeping officially switched to Coordinated Universal Time, marked by atomic clocks. **Cesium** clocks keep time accurately to 30 billionths of a second per

1972

Coordinated Universal Time, which uses atomic clocks, gets its start.

President Richard Nixon visits China.

year. The Bureau of International Time in France keeps time zones **synchronized** with the world's atomic clocks.

Sidereal time is another method of measuring astronomical time. It is based on the movement of stars in our sky. A sidereal day lasts 23 hours, 56 minutes, and 4.09 seconds. It measures the time it takes for a specific star to orbit the Earth completely.

TWO MORE CALENDARS?

Forty calendars are in use around the world today. Yet each has its problems. Scientists and mathematicians have considered the possibilities of using one of two new calendars—the International Fixed Calendar or the World Calendar.

The International Fixed Calendar would be a **perpetual**

28

2000

The new millennium is officially celebrated (left).

George W. Bush and Al Gore run in the presidential election.

Gregorian calendar of thirteen months, with twenty-eight days each. All months would begin on a Sunday and end on a Saturday. Every fourth year, a leap day would follow June 28.

Another possible calendar is the World Calendar. This calendar would divide years into four quarters of ninety-one days each, plus one day at the end of each year. The first month of every quarter would have thirty-one days. The second and third months would have thirty days. January 1, April 1, July 1, and October 1 would be the first days of the quarters, and each would fall on a Sunday.

No one knows how we will record days and months in the future. Perhaps, we won't even have days and months. We'll have to wait and see.

2001

The new millennium really begins.

Harry Potter and the Sorcerer's Stone (right) opens in movie theaters.

2012

The Maya Great Cycle ends.

29

astronomer (uh-STRON-uh-muhr)
An astronomer is a person who studies the stars and planets. The astronomer Sosigenes devised a new calendar for Julius Caesar.

celestial (suh-LESS-chuhl)
Celestial events are happenings in the sky or heavens. The Julian count helps astronomers determine the time between two major celestial events.

cesium (SEE-zee-uhm)
Cesium is a radioactive element used in atomic time. Cesium clocks measure time accurately to 30 billionths of a second per year.

constellation (kon-stuh-LAY-shuhn)
A constellation is a pattern of stars, usually connected to animals or to myths. Sirius is a star in the constellation Canis Major.

eclipses (i-KLIPS-ez)
Eclipses occur when the moon passes between the Earth and the sun, or when the sun passes between the Earth and the moon. Major celestial events include eclipses and passing comets.

lunar (LOO-nur)
Lunar events are related to the moon. A calendar based on the moon's cycle is a lunar calendar.

perpetual (pur-PECH-oo-uhl)
Perpetual activity continues without ever stopping. A perpetual calendar does not need to be reset.

pictograph (PIK-toh-graf)
A pictograph is a picture used to represent an event or person. Pictographs appear on Plains Indian winter counts.

solar (SOH-lur)
Solar events are related to the sun. A solar calendar is based on Earth's revolution around the sun.

synchronized (SING-kruh-nized)
Synchronized events are timed to happen together. Synchronized clocks tell exactly the same time.

tropical year (TROP-uh-kuhl YIHR)
A tropical year is measured as it occurs along the equator. The length of the tropical year is used to determine an accurate calendar.

vectors (VEHK-tuhrz)
Vectors are courses or compass directions, or lines running along such courses. Vectors connecting stone piles on a medicine wheel point to stars.

zodiac (ZOH-dee-ak)
The zodiac is an imaginary group of animals and figures connected to constellations. The Chinese zodiac includes twelve.

FOR FURTHER INFORMATION

AT THE LIBRARY

Nonfiction

*Branley, Franklyn, and Jill Weber (illustrator). *Keeping Time.* Boston: Houghton Mifflin, 1993.

George, Lynn. *Calendars of Native Americans: Timekeeping Methods of Ancient North America.* New York: PowerKids Press, 2004.

Maestro, Betsy. *The Story of Clocks and Calendars: Marking a Millennium.* New York: Lothrop, Lee & Shepard, 1999.

*Richards, E. G. *Mapping Time: The Calendar and Its History.* New York: Oxford University Press, 1998.

Skurzynski, Gloria. *On Time: From Seasons to Split Seconds.* Washington, D.C.: National Geographic Society, 2000.

Fiction

Scieszka, Jon, and Adam McCauley (illustrator). *Me Oh Maya!* New York: Viking, 2003.

Books marked with a star are challenge reading material for those reading above grade level.

ON THE WEB

Visit our home page for lots of links about calendars:
http://www.childsworld.com/links

Note to Parents, Teachers, and Librarians:
We routinely check our Web links to make sure they're safe, active sites—so encourage your readers to check them out!

PLACES TO VISIT OR CONTACT

Frank H. McClung Museum, University of Tennessee
1327 Circle Park Drive
Knoxville, TN 37996
865/974-2144

Wanuskewin Heritage Park
RR #4
Saskatoon, Saskatchewan
S7K 3J7
Canada
306/931-6767

INDEX

ABOUT THE AUTHOR

BARBARA SOMERVILL IS THE AUTHOR OF MANY BOOKS FOR CHILDREN.
SHE LOVES LEARNING AND SEES EVERY WRITING PROJECT AS A CHANCE
TO LEARN NEW INFORMATION OR GAIN A NEW UNDERSTANDING.
MS. SOMERVILL GREW UP IN NEW YORK STATE, BUT HAS ALSO LIVED
IN TORONTO, CANADA; CANBERRA, AUSTRALIA; CALIFORNIA; AND
SOUTH CAROLINA. SHE CURRENTLY LIVES WITH HER HUSBAND IN
SIMPSONVILLE, SOUTH CAROLINA.